Self-Coaching Essentials

A Handbook for Achieving Exceptional Results

R. Sean Cochran

Copyright © 2014 R. Sean Cochran

All rights reserved.

CONTENTS

1	Coaching and Self-Coaching	3
2	Where Can You Kill?	13
3	Getting Your Stories Straight	21
4	No One is Coming	29
5	In the Path of the Idea Stream	37
6	Sprints and Marathons	43
7	Villages and Villagers	53
8	Fear and Courage	63
9	Recording in HD	71
10	Simple Stuff	81

ACKNOWLEDGMENTS

This book is a collection of observations gleaned from having worked with some of the top financial services professionals in the world. Without your collaboration and guidance I would have no insights at all, nor would this book be possible. Thank you for allowing me to learn from you and in some cases for permitting me to be your coach. It has been an honor.

I would also like to acknowledge my father, Richard T. Cochran. You have been a professional mentor to me for many years. You have also managed to build a world in which you exercise your signature strengths every day in service of your clients, colleagues and family. That is really what this book is all about.

CHAPTER 1

COACHING AND SELF-COACHING

"Our plans miscarry because they have no aim. When a man does not know what harbor he is making for, no wind is the right wind."

- *Seneca*

So why does anyone need coaching? For most of us, life is pretty good as it is. On average we tend to have our "up" days, our "down" days, and we learn along the way as we travel through life. Every year we get a little wiser with experience and life is our coach. So why would we need further coaching?

Is coaching for individuals who are struggling in life? Or perhaps it's for eccentrics who read too many self-help books and can't seem to accomplish anything?

Coaching is an investment in yourself, and if you look around more carefully you begin to see that top-performers in any field tend to make such an investment.

Why do professional athletes have coaches? Athletes at the top of their game, including those who are the best in the world at their sport, have coaches. And they don't necessarily seek out coaches who are more skilled than they are in their chosen sport. They look for coaches to serve a different purpose and they understand a subtle secret, namely that coaching is more about the person being coached than the coach. Personal coaching is about *you* and a coach is simply there to help you engage with *yourself*.

Have you ever worked out with a personal trainer? Most of us intuitively know how to lift heavy objects, and gaining a more nuanced understanding of workout routines does not take long, yet having a personal trainer *works*. It causes you to show up, it helps you to persist, it encourages you to push a little harder, and it raises your level of pride as you progress. With a trainer you are visible, you are accountable, and you are forced to be honest with yourself. But your trainer isn't lifting your weights for you and the trainer doesn't drive you to the gym. You have allowed the trainer to hold you accountable and you have given them the *authority* to push you and direct you because you know it's in your best interest.

Can you coach yourself?

This book is about self-coaching, and I believe that we can coach ourselves, but first we need to understand ourselves a little better. Let me introduce you to two different "selves" that live in your head.

Your strategic-self

Your strategic self is the part of you that sits down and devises plans. If you are engaging in a workout program, it was the strategic-self that bought the package and designed the workout schedule. Your strategic-self realized that if you went to the gym three days a week then you would lose weight and look good, and so a plan was born. The strategic-self did the math and realized that you'd have to wake up at 5:30am (rather than at 7:00am) in order to have time to exercise, shower and head to the office. That was the plan. The problem is that your strategic-self made the plan but this version of you won't be the one executing the plan.

Your execution-self

Your alarm just went off. It's early. In fact it feels ungodly early and the snooze button looks great. One snooze won't hurt, right? In fact, you can still squeeze in a short workout if you hit the snooze button twice. Actually, who works out this early anyway!? Your job is important, and you really do need your sleep. Maybe we'll start tomorrow?

This is your execution-self. Your strategic-self crafted the plan, but you're experiencing some personal insubordination and your execution-self doesn't want to comply with your strategic-self's directive.

Having a coach can fix this problem. On some level you know that if you had a coach next to you in the morning with a whistle and a megaphone to force you out of bed then you'd be better off for it. That's what coaches do. They've been given the authority to kick your butt out of bed. They are agents of your strategic-self and they force your execution-self to deliver.

A stern discussion with your selves

For self-coaching to work, you need to have a conversation with your selves, right now. This book will help your strategic-self establish plans that will improve your quality of life and your financial situation, but only if you don't allow personal insubordination. You need to look in the mirror and give your strategic-self the authority to command your execution-self. Hand the strategic-self the coaching whistle and the megaphone and simply commit to using them ruthlessly on your execution-self. I'm dead serious, and this really works.

If the strategic-self has made a plan, then look in the mirror and straighten your execution-self out. If it involves 5:30am wakeup calls then so be it. Your execution-self is going to have to deliver. This doesn't mean that your strategic-self can't alter the plan. However, don't allow for plan alterations when you in fact know that your execution-self is behind the steering wheel. How do you know who is driving? If it's 5:30am and your alarm just went off then it's a pretty good bet that it's your execution-self that's tired and looking for plan B.

My own story

Before we go much further, I should tell you a little more about my own story. I started my professional career in 1997 as a private wealth management client advisor in Columbus, Ohio. My father is a client advisor as well and I viewed this path to be the family business and moved in this direction with a degree of pride and family camaraderie. I enjoyed advising clients and after a few years I decided to lift my technical skills and moved to New York City to pursue an MBA at Columbia Business School. Thereafter, I stayed in New York and eventually shifted my focus to work with international clients who live offshore but hold assets in the United States.

Over time I realized that my greatest strengths were in coaching and presenting to our firm's clients and to other client advisor colleagues. Accordingly, my organization eventually invited me to work as a consultant to other offshore client advisors, a role which catered to these strengths. I then began to partner with client advisors, coaching them on their delivery of wealth management services and on growing their businesses.

When this consulting function was extended to Asia in 2007 I relocated to support our colleagues in the region. And so I soon found myself living in Singapore leading a team of coaches and consultants and supporting wealth management client advisors throughout Asia. I spent the next 6 years flying into the Philippines, Thailand, India, Malaysia, and other Asian countries, educating clients on wealth management and coaching client advisors on the growth of their practices.

I later moved to Sydney in 2012, where I currently reside and where I continue to provide similar coaching for client advisors in Australia. In 2014 I will now move once again, this time to Hong Kong where I will take on similar coaching responsibilities.

This book draws from these life experiences and my time spent as a professional coach, salesperson, and presenter to hundreds of client advisors and thousands of clients. I have spent my career within the private wealth management industry, but this is not a book about wealth management. It is a book of lessons gleaned while working with top professionals to support the achievement of their goals.

I've been extraordinarily fortunate to have been able to observe and work with some of the most successful financial professionals in the world. In my presentations I often comment that most of my insights are not my own, but come from the individuals I work with. I have been well positioned to observe top performers and spend my time collecting their hard earned insights and sharing them with others. As a coach, I like to think I've played a role in the success of some of them along the way, but I am fundamentally an observer and hope to now share these observations with you.

What will you do with this information?

This book aims to have a particular focus on *actions*. There is a wide gulf between having an epiphany, and turning that epiphany into *actions*. How many times have you listened to a presentation, nodded your head in agreement and walked away with insights only to later realize that you never *did* anything with the information? I think it happens all the time. We think, "That's a good idea…. I fully agree…. I need to remember that….", but we fail to turn these sentiments into concrete *actions*.

At the end of each chapter, you will see a list of questions to help you think about the topics raised. You will also find *specific action items to encourage* you to do something with the information. You'll be tempted to skip over this part to keep moving through the content. Fight the temptation to simply read through and try to actually force yourself to take the prescribed actions. Intuitively thinking that you've gained an insight is different than forcing yourself to write down what you intend to do with it. Then when you finish the book, keep these commitments visible so that they can serve as reminders to you. Hold yourself accountable and give self-coaching a shot.

Questions

Think about the following...

1) Have you ever had a coach add value to some aspect of your life?
2) Would you like to be able to coach *yourself* to achieve your goals?
3) Is your strategic-self effective in selecting goals and designing plans to achieve them?
4) Does your execution-self deliver on those plans in order to achieve the goals?

Actions

What are you going to do with this information...

1) As you go through this book, commit yourself to writing down potential *actions* after each chapter.
2) Ensure that your strategic-self has the authority to direct your execution-self. It is your *execution*-self that needs to deliver on the actions as you proceed.
3) This is a book on *self*-coaching, but having someone external to observe your journey through these pages can't hurt. Consider telling someone what you intend to do with this information after each chapter. Writing actions down and telling someone what they are may help you to execute.

R. Sean Cochran

CHAPTER 2

WHERE CAN YOU KILL?

"A winner is someone who recognizes his God-given talents, works his tail off to develop them into skills, and uses these skills to accomplish his goals."

- *Larry Bird*

Before you can coach yourself or be coached by another person, you have to get clear on what equation you are optimizing. In other words, what is the point? What does winning look like? Can you imagine a sports coach working productively with clients without an understanding of what winning looks like? There is also a distinct difference between understanding how to win and understanding why you play a particular game (as opposed to some other game) and why you play at all. If you are a basketball player, it first needs to be clear how you play the game if you are to get any good at it. However, if you move to a higher level of analysis you can ask yourself why you might play basketball rather than baseball. Or you can ask why you play sports at all.

It's not helpful to engage in metaphysical thought in the midst of the big game, but you really should reflect on such issues at some point. These are your foundations, and unfortunately there are plenty of individuals who end up getting quite skilled at "games" (careers, pursuits, and entire lives) they get no satisfaction from playing.

Well-being is the point

I believe the only rational starting point is to begin with the assertion that we ought to be optimizing our *well-being*. This might sound simple, but we don't always behave in ways that optimize well-being so it's worth gaining a better understanding of the equation. The literature on personal well-being grows more robust by the day and the field of "positive psychology" is pioneering a greater understanding of what leads to human well-being in actual practice (the answers are not always intuitive). The field is young and it seems that most psychology fields have focused their emphasis on curing *negative* psychology rather than maximizing *positive* psychology. However, this is changing and there are volumes now being produced on the topic to attest to this renaissance.

An equation for well-being

The clearest articulation of an equation for well-being equation comes from psychologist Martin Seligman and he asserts that well-being consists of the following 5 elements[1]:

1) Positive Emotion

2) Engagement

3) Relationships

---

[1] Martin Seligman, *Flourish* (Free Press, 2011)

4) Meaning

5) Achievement

These 5 factors constitute and create well-being and as we drive them higher we in turn drive our well-being higher. Having a categorization like this is useful in that we can take each factor and consider where we stand and how we can improve it in order to improve the quality of our lives. We can also consider which goals are consistent with driving the factors higher and whether some goals may not be justifiable if well-being is to be the underlying driver of our value system.

Signature strengths

Perhaps one of the most important takeaways from Dr. Seligman (from a coaching perspective) is the further insight that these 5 factors tie into the recognition, development, and practice of our personal "signature strengths". By cultivating and exercising our signature strengths we are able to achieve more positive emotion, higher levels of engagement, deeper relationships, greater meaning and stronger achievement.

It follows that one of the most important things we can possibly do in our lives is to understand, cultivate, and exercise our signature strengths. We need an accurate inventory of what those strengths are and we should align our lives, careers, and goals to those signature strengths.

Many life coaches, performance coaches, and executive coaches have used this insight as one of the foundations of their practice and as a means of encouraging higher levels of achievement. You need to take the time to understand what your strengths truly are and then invest in going from a position of strength to a position of dominance.

Having coached some of the top financial client advisors in the world for many years, I can tell you that I've seen this principle in practice. I'll make a controversial statement, but one that I've come to believe, namely that beyond a certain level of seniority I believe that coaching areas of *weakness* is largely a waste of time. Let me explain.

Scenario 1:

You have identified certain areas in your life where you have "gaps". You notice that you dislike working on these areas and when faced with related challenges you often procrastinate rather than charge forward. You feel that for the sake of your development you should improve these areas of weakness and your employer is encouraging development programs to make you more well-rounded.

Scenario 2:

You have identified certain areas in your life where you have outlier strengths. You notice that you like working on them and when faced with related challenges you typically charge forward rather than procrastinate. You feel that for the sake of your development you should develop these areas of *strength*. In your professional life you focus energy on these strengths and seek to outsource your areas of weakness to others who are stronger in these areas.

In my experience, *most winners are following scenario 2*.

If you are new to an industry and have certain very basic knowledge gaps then of course you need to build the foundations that are required. However, beyond that baseline you are far better served by committing to scenario 2.

In scenario 2 you can take on massive challenges, yet wake up energized and ready to conquer the world. Time passes quickly, your pride grows explosively, and you see exponential returns to your well-being and likely to your finances.

In scenario 1, you'll improve your weaknesses and become more well-rounded, but it won't be fun and if you manage to press through and improve your "gaps" you run the greatest risk of all. You might get good at things you simply don't want to do. Waking up to a job in which you've become good at things you don't want to do is a recipe for personal crisis. This is tragic. Don't do it.

What are your signature strengths?

Signature strengths are best viewed as fundamental, rather than activity-specific or industry-specific. For example, you may have the ability to work well with accounting spreadsheets, but the signature strengths behind this may involve a love of quantitative analysis, an appreciation for detail, and a love for problem solving in a game with consistent rules.

I have also seen attempts to delineate signature strengths at levels that are too general to be applicable. For example, I have a "love of learning", but the truth is I love learning some things a little more than others and learning can take many shapes. Therefore identification of "love of learning" as a signature strength might be a little too broad to be useful.

Many of us spend too little time taking inventory and end up crafting lives that are not designed with the expression of signature strengths as an underlying priority. We become relatively skilled in areas where we lack true differentiated strength and we risk pressing on in an unengaged state.

Of course, we all need to gain sufficient exposure to the world in order to sufficiently understand which activities might satisfy the expression of our strengths. We will also face a learning curve in new pursuits and early learning is not the same thing as rectifying known weakness. For the purposes of this book, I assume the reader to be at a developmental stage having had sufficiently broad exposure to be able to make an informed determination of personal strengths and weaknesses.

Questions

Think about the following...

1) What activities make you lose track of time in a fully engaged state? These activities may imply you are exercising an underlying signature strength.
2) Are there areas where others recognize your skills to be highly differentiated? These areas are likely leveraging your signature strengths.
3) Are there activities you dread participating in and which cause you anxiety and frustration well in advance of the start of the activity? These are not likely to be aligned to signature strengths.
4) Does your life and your chosen career line up with your signature strengths? Could it be better aligned?

Actions

What are you going to do with this information...

1) Write down a few of your signature strengths.
2) Write down professions, roles, or projects that align to your signature strengths. Even if you are currently well-aligned to your strengths, identify how you might leverage your strengths more fully on a daily basis.
3) Write down a couple weaknesses that you've been working to improve. Where possible, redirect energy toward compounding strengths rather than on remediating weakness.

As we progress into building your story and establishing goals, you need to bear these strengths in mind. At all costs, make sure you don't get good at things you don't want to do and that you don't move quickly into a life you don't want to lead. Live on purpose and design strategies (and goals) that improve your well-being and align to your strengths.

CHAPTER 3

GETTING YOUR STORIES STRAIGHT

"The world is full of people who know the price of everything and the value of nothing."

- Oscar Wilde

Once you have identified your signature strengths, you will need to focus on defining your "story". This exercise is about *value proposition* on varying different levels. Without a clear understanding of your strengths this exercise is difficult as you won't be able to articulate differentiated value when such value is only loosely understood. However, the exercises are iterative in that often you may have some conception of signature strengths, but it is only when you take the time to craft your "story" that you come to fully recognize differentiated value with full clarity.

Your "story" consists of the answers to these questions:

What do you do?

How do you do what you do?

Why are you different?

Who do you do it for?

These are all value proposition stories, and I use the term "story" to signify that you need to not only understand the answer but also *how to say the answer with conviction and authenticity*. You do not need to be an actor or showman, but you do need to be *authentic* as a communicator. The world (starting with you) needs to know and understand your value and this requires that you are able to express these points without hesitation as though you've made these points so many times that the task no longer requires skill of recall. You need to own the answers and they must come out of you in an authentic voice. This is what it means to "get your stories straight". The stories become who you are and your identity is actually strengthened and affirmed in this process.

Your story expresses your differentiated value and sets you on your way to aligning your life to your strengths.

What do you do?

The answer to this question is often unrehearsed because on some level we each feel as though we know what we do and can answer "on-the-fly" when asked. We think to ourselves, "this is about me, and I know 'me' very well and have better things to memorize".

No matter how well we feel we know ourselves, the outside world *hears* our message, *sees* our body language, and *feels* our conviction. Others don't have access to our inner worlds. We also tend to overestimate the degree to which we really know ourselves and the refinement of this answer helps us gain *clarity of self* and not simply greater skill in communication.

Take the time to craft the answer to this question and draft it into one or two *written* sentences. Work on this statement until you feel it expresses what you do in as few words as possible while retaining the message.

Now state the answer *out loud*. You don't want to stutter or struggle to recall information. You also don't want to seem as though you are mechanically delivering a speech. Realize that others can detect even a millisecond of hesitation if you struggle to recall information. With practice you'll move past this early phase and you'll identify with and own the message. It should eventually come out as though it's simply you. This is what authenticity sounds like and this is where you need to be.

How do you do what you do?

Once someone knows what you do, they may ask a follow on question to find out what *exactly* you do. How do you perform your role *in practice* and can you say a little more about your *process*. When others scratch one inch below your surface there needs to be more to your story which you can readily share.

You don't need to be "6 feet deep", but you need to have more to reveal if someone goes a few inches below the surface. With advisors and specialists I've worked with, I often point out that people (often wrongly) assume that if your knowledge exceeds their depth then you are "bottomless" in expertise. In other words, if your audience has "3 inches of understanding" and you demonstrate "4 inches of knowledge" then you will be assumed to have bottomless depth. Whether you are required to have 6 inches or 12 feet of knowledge is a question for your profession to answer, but from a pure communication standpoint you need not be concerned that you are not infinitely deep. Generally speaking your audience won't probe as far as you fear they will.

Take the time to craft a few sentences on your process. "How do you do what you do?" Now consider asking a trusted friend or colleague what they think of your delivery. Is it natural and authentic?

Why are you different?

Your audience is usually unable to differentiate between you and others who profess to do what you do. If you have worked on the responses to "what you do" and "how you do it" then perhaps you sound and seem confident, but it's also important to be *differentiated*.[2]

The most common error I've seen here is the tendency to focus on a multitude of points rather than selecting a couple points of clear differentiation. Colleagues *in your field* have a greater attention span for your response to this question and the ability to discern nuanced

---

[2] The best treatment I have seen on articulating a differentiated personal value proposition comes from Leo Pusateri, President of Pusateri Consulting and Training. Refer to his book, "Mirror Mirror on the Wall Am I the Most Valued of Them All?" for an excellent discussion of this topic.

differentiation. Everyone else will only understand or recall a couple points. And they'd better be simple.

I have a colleague who made a brilliant point on differentiation by asserting that "if your clients are not referring others to you it means they don't know what to say about you when you aren't in the room". I think this is profound and true.

Ask yourself, what do people say about you when you aren't in the room? They will not articulate a multitude of small, nuanced points. They will make one or two statements that they feel broadly characterize you. They'll also make mention of you when those simple points are relevant to a conversation. Don't leave these points up to chance, and don't allow others to create their own script when you have the power to influence it.

Some colleagues have asked how to craft differentiation points if they are in fact *"well-rounded generalists"*. My answer is that they should reconsider their branding and look harder for differentiation. It is not likely that others are referring to you as "well-rounded" and if they are then this won't likely be a memorable personal brand to present to the world.

Take the time to craft a couple of differentiation statements for yourself. Make them simple and think of them as the two sentences you want your clients, colleagues, and friends to say about you when you are not in the room.

Who do you do it for?

We sometimes blur the lines between specializing in a particular *type of service* as opposed to specializing in the needs of a particular *type of client*. This question asks about the *type of client* you serve. As you respond to this question the listener will file your response in their mind and use it to determine whether what you do is relevant to them or to others they know. You want to be front of mind for the right clients and excluded from consideration by those who don't fit the profile. Your answer to this question matters because your listener is thinking about who they will tell about you.

Which clients or markets are best suited to what you do, your process, and your differentiated value?

Which clients or markets would you like to avoid?

You want to be the logical choice such that if someone knows of a client that meets the criteria of your segment then they'll be inclined to tell them about you. You want your audience to think, "...my cousin fits that description and your *specialized* focus would be of interest. Maybe I should tell him about you". Take the time to think through your response to this question, bearing these considerations in mind.

As a final point, note that although you are crafting "stories and narratives" in this section, you are also refining your self-understanding. If you don't have these stories on the tip of your tongue then it likely means that further reflection is warranted. That reflection is not simply a matter of thinking about how to say concepts you currently know. Often you will find that you gain truly greater clarity of the concepts themselves by forcing this exercise. You will get to know yourself more intimately than before and may even actively define yourself as you proceed.

Questions

Think about the following...

1) What do you think people say about you when you are not in the room? This is your personal brand, and you have one whether you like it or not.
2) How well do you know the answer to the four questions raised in this chapter?
3) What do you look like and sound like when you express these stories out loud?

Actions

What are you going to do with this information...

1) Answer the following questions in writing:
   o *What do you do?*

   o *How do you do what you do?*

   o *Why are you different?*

   o *Who do you do it for?*

2) Now answer these questions out loud. This is the *delivery of your story*. How do you think you sound? Do you hesitate? Are you authentic?
3) Now have someone listen to you deliver your stories. How do they think you sound and appear? This is the *perception of your story*.

Take an active role in designing your personal brand or the world will craft this brand for you.

CHAPTER 4

NO ONE IS COMING

"People are always blaming their circumstances for what they are. I don't believe in circumstances. The people who get on in the world are the people who get up and look for the circumstances they want, and if they can't find them, make them."

- George Bernard Shaw

Randomness

Without having to take inventory or investigate, I'm certain I know a few of the people in your office. Some of them can't wait to corner you for a conversation on how all of the successful professionals around them are simply *lucky*.

"It must be nice…" is a common refrain, and they feel as though as long as they can't see the chain of causation that led to success, it must be random luck.

"He inherited most of his clients…"

"He was promoted because of his relationship with ABC…"

"The other division always refers to colleague X…"

Some take this step a bit further and revel in another level of this disease. Some feel that not only are successful colleagues *lucky* but they themselves are *victims*. There is a strange catharsis surrounding the activity of describing the injustices of the world around the water cooler. These colleagues will also be quick to find each other because it seems to be more satisfying to describe one's victimhood around others who compound the sentiment.

Don't fall into this trap. This is a disempowering place to live, and worse yet, it's misguided.

I don't believe in randomness.

What appears to be luck is almost always the result of replicable measures if you scratch beneath the surface. For example, if someone seems to always get referrals from within the company then perhaps you should ask yourself how they came to have the sort of internal networks that yields this result. Why do others feel comfortable sending business to them? Why are they "top of mind"? What are they doing (not only now but perhaps years ago) to create these circumstances? If you look more closely you can almost always find the chain of causation. And that chain of causation is very often something that you can replicate.

Victimization

The "victim mindset" is even more insidious because at least randomness can work in your favor from time to time. If you've spent too long in the "victim mindset" then you start to believe that the universe is conspiring against you. In fact as you begin to learn that this is not the case, you may *miss* having the ability to commiserate with others who still feel victimized! For some reason there is an emotional release in the mental state of righteous indignation. The problem is that these states share in common the notion that you do not and cannot control your environment or that you are waiting for someone or something to fix the situation.

"Management needs to do something about this..."

What if you assumed that *no one is coming*? Better yet, what if you didn't need or want someone to come and sort things out?

Control your variables

If you start with the assumption that there is no randomness, that you control your variables, and that "no one is coming" to sort this out for you, then you are in the most highly empowered state. It means you are on the path to controlling your future.

To live in a world where no one is coming requires that you think a little harder about variables and about the actions you take and the scenarios you can control. Many who are waiting for someone to come and assign them tasks will end up with exactly that, *assigned* tasks. If you do not design your own environment then you risk floating adrift looking for a captain or having others build your world for you.

Let me give an example. I had a manager recently who came to me and described how his direct report was extremely skilled in various areas, but he was going home early due to lack of engagement in his role. This manager's staff member recalled times in his life when he worked late and felt driven and now found himself under-utilized. The line manager sought my advice on how we might better utilize this resource.

In a corporate environment we can fail to appreciate that we are able to act as entrepreneurs *as long as we exercise this ability*. This manager's staff member will likely soon have a list of tasks created (by others) in order to keep him engaged and although he'll be busier, his ability to control his variables will diminish.

Alternatively, if we each review our environment and assume that *no one is coming*, that no tasks will be assigned, that no one will make our work more interesting, and that no one else will build a master plan, then we start to assume responsibility and exert control *ourselves*.

Create your own projects, align them to your signature strengths, create milestones for the success of those projects and tell your manager what you intend to do. If you don't make the first move then someone may actually come and do it for you. Assume no one is coming and move with enough speed that when they do come you're already engaged in a project that adds value to your company and enriches your own life.

I've gone through similar steps in our firm's internal personal development planning process. My organization has an institutionalized process whereby staff are invited to articulate career ambitions and then highlight intermediary development goals to support attainment of those ambitions. There are two ways to go about this exercise.

One way to go about the exercise is to articulate career goals and then to indicate to your manager the requirements you have in order to achieve those goals. These requirements may entail the organization providing financial support for training, securing a mentor for you, assigning certain projects of relevance and so on.

Another way to go about the exercise is to articulate career goals and to then describe to your manager the steps that *you will be taking* in order to develop yourself regardless of what the organization supports. In this alternative, you highlight what *you* are going to do. You only seek validation from the firm that the steps you are taking *on your own* are agreed to be consistent with the career path you've described. This version doesn't ask for anything and it's even more powerful if you head into the meeting having already achieved certain of the intermediary goals. Perhaps you've already enlisted someone as your mentor, you've already created a project that develops your skills, and you booked a flight (potentially on personal expense) to another branch to meet professionals important to your network. What kind of impression do you think this version makes? How empowering do you think it feels?

I've given examples from within a corporate context, but this is even more straightforward in an entrepreneurial setting. Wring out the randomness and make the first moves in your life. Don't wait for someone to come, and if you're smart you'll act before anyone else can get there!

Questions

Think about the following...

1) Do you feel that your success depends on *you*, or have you been focusing on the variables and people around you?
2) Do you believe in randomness and generally attribute success in others to luck?
3) How carefully do you really look for causation and control before you attribute situations to randomness?
4) Do you have a career development plan? More importantly, have you shared that plan with your line manager, your colleagues, or with the Human Resources department? Don't allow this to be invisible.

Actions

What are you going to do with this information...

1) Commit to looking deeply at causal effects. For example, if you believe you failed because a manager simply didn't like you, ask yourself why that was the case and what you could have done which might have altered that fact. Causal chains are *always* there and most variables are in fact within your control if you dig.
2) Deconstruct a particular failure or conflict and identify what *you yourself* might have done differently. Define your world in terms of *your* decisions, and not in terms of the results of the decisions and actions of others.
3) Create a *written* personal career development plan. Let other stakeholders know about it and let it drive your actions. It will ultimately guide *their* actions as well. Don't wait for others to plan your career for you.

R. Sean Cochran

CHAPTER 5

IN THE PATH OF THE IDEA STREAM

"Creativity is just connecting things. When you ask creative people how they did something, they feel a little guilty because they didn't really do it, they just saw something. It seemed obvious to them after a while."

- Steve Jobs

If you are determined to take control of your destiny and shape the environment around you, you need to make sure you have creative *content*. An entrepreneurial spirit and an attitude of empowerment are necessary but far from sufficient for outlier success. Once you have determined that you will chart your own course, you have to make sure your mind is fertile enough to blaze the trail and that you can originate high quality ideas.

There are some individuals who appear extremely creative and who seem to constantly have good ideas and the ability to paint compelling visions of the future. Some people genuinely do have outlier ability in certain creative areas, but it's also often the case that they simply know how to put themselves *"in the path of the idea stream"*.

Our ideas do not come out of nowhere and magically spark themselves to life. They come from our minds and the fertility of our minds, and our ability to cultivate ideas from our own minds, can be greatly influenced. The key is to have an appreciation for the magnitude of our own ignorance and to systematically ensure that *outside* sources of insight make their way to us. I may not know what my next great idea will be, but if I place myself in the path of a stream of ideas then I can be assured that some derivative of what I am absorbing will grow into future insights. So what are some potential ways to do this?

I recall when eBooks and Kindle reading devices first became popular. I vehemently insisted that I did not want such a device and that I believed books ought to be printed on *paper*. I love books and I love bookstores and there is a romance to both. One Christmas my mother bought me a Kindle as she had not yet heard my rant on the romance of *real* books and *physical* bookstores, and this turned out to be a pivotal moment. It's true that I still love real books and physical bookstores. It is also true that I probably read more than *triple* the amount of content due to the fact that I can download any book on any topic within seconds, and can do so at a fraction of the price.

Such reading habits can be a tremendous means of placing yourself in the path of the idea stream, but you need to systematize a regular pattern. The real breakthrough for me personally was a determination that I would read every morning for 30-45 minutes at a scheduled time before going to work. I also determined to download multiple books at a time, and to focus the content around the nature of thinking that would best carry me forward given current projects. This may seem simple and intuitive, but in actual practice a committed routine can make a big difference. It's much like determining that you will have a regular and systematic workout pattern. Any single workout is only barely relevant, but the accumulation of a year's worth of discipline can bear fruit.

There is also a discipline required around the nature of one's reading if it is for the purpose of remaining in the path of the idea stream. For example, I am terribly undisciplined when it comes to swimming for the sake of exercise. When I get near the pool my thoughts turn to pina coladas and lounging around on a floating device. As my wife is quick to point out, not all "swimming" is created equal when it comes to swimming routines for workout purposes. IPads and Kindles run the same risk when you have your email, the internet, Angry Birds, and other diversions readily available on your reading device. And while reading the romance novel "50 Shades of Grey" is perfectly fine for recreation, it is not the sort of reading likely to foster a flow of creative professional ideas.

Another means of keeping yourself in the flow of the idea stream is to watch high quality speakers in action. For example, consider watching what are known as "TED Talks". TED stands for "Technology, Entertainment, and Design" and there are "TED Conferences" organized around the world to showcase the top minds in these and other fields. Each speaker is given only 18 minutes to speak and they are disciplined in keeping to this allotted time.

The preparation that speakers invest in these talks is highly evident and the tight time budget ensures that they reach their point concisely. All of these talks are uploaded to YouTube and can be viewed on the internet for free. The first time you stumble onto some of these talks you will likely be blown away by the quality of the content and the caliber of the speakers. These talks can be useful on their own, or if you are reading a book that fascinates you by an author well known in their field then it's worth a look to see whether the author has a TED talk. Often they do.

If you work in a multi-national corporation then another way of remaining in the idea stream is to determine what others in your organization are doing in various locations around the world. I recall that while working in Australia I had uncovered a particular training program in Phoenix, Arizona and when I phoned the organizers they were more than happy to permit me to join the program. I paid for the flights on personal expense but the value I derived was so great that it far exceeded the costs of this investment.

There are decidedly hundreds of ways one might ensure that the ingredients for creative thought are in close proximity, but the key is to *systematize* the practice. I don't know which ideas will stick for you or which concepts will end up sparking the insights that could lead to major leaps forward. I do know that if you systematically place yourself in the path of the idea stream then your chances of originating and then compounding those insights goes up dramatically.

Questions

Think about the following...

1) Are you placing yourself in the path of the idea stream? Don't get lulled into thinking you have all the insight you need. Don't fail to appreciate the magnitude of what you don't know.
2) What are your idea sources? Are they of the right quality, quantity, and diversity?
3) Do you have a *systematic* pattern for gaining insight from these sources?
4) What training opportunities do you have access to? What training opportunities *could* you gain access to?
5) Are you willing to invest in yourself?

Actions

What are you going to do with this information...

1) Buy an eBook reading device (e.g., Kindle, iPad, Nook) and fill it with books on topics that enrich your creativity and understanding. Select topics aligned to existing strengths as well as topics that can magnify your skills.
2) Learn about TED talks and listen to the brightest minds in various fields.
3) Establish exactly *when* you'll do your reading and watching when it comes to this content. You need a *systematic* practice and the discipline to stick with it.
4) If you work for a corporate employer, commit to exploring what training your company has to offer and don't hesitate to personally invest in yourself.

CHAPTER 6

SPRINTS AND MARATHONS

"Nothing is particularly hard if you divide it into small jobs."

- Henry Ford

During college I remember a conversation with a trusted friend who challenged me on my perspective. I was asked, *"Don't you think you need to live in the 'real' world?"*

He asked this question because at that time I was pursuing a personal goal and I had elevated its importance in my mind to an almost religious place. I find that when you have goals that feel overwhelmingly important you live life with a focused sense of purpose which guides your actions like a compass. When you live with a less emotionally charged task list, life simply has less flavor. There is nothing quite as motivating as having a goal that you are able to elevate to a surreal place in your world.

The unfortunate truth is that most of us have relatively few goals at that level of importance. We tend to have task lists and a set of roughly defined values in our subconscious. We go about our days executing tasks and on occasion we get a bit more enthused when they align closely to values and strengths. This is the "real" world for many.

At the same time, we look on in envy at those who are on their way to achieving some higher purpose. When we watch a movie about someone relentlessly working to be the best in their field we feel inspired. When we see sports teams struggling to achieve victory we feel moved. On some level we connect because we understand that there is simply something magical about the pursuit of a meaningful goal.

So why do we need to live in the "real" world, devoid of magic? Why not live in a world in which we are constantly on a mission? It feels better to live in a world in which we are pursuing something with enough purpose to filter and guide our actions. Actions consistent with the goal are filtered *in* and actions inconsistent with the goal are filtered *out*. Someone with goals such as this is able to achieve amazing things because a conscious (and subconscious) clarity of purpose is able to guide decisions and actions in alignment.

The reality is that we tend to wait for goals to choose us rather than the other way around. We may also believe that a select few have discovered they possess certain natural gifts and are nearly compelled by nature to pursue them. This view is self-limiting as it implies that one cannot simply *self-generate* a higher sense of purpose and get to work on creating the magic. I strongly believe we can.

We've gone through the exercise of determining signature strengths and using them to guide our path forward. This exercise itself is the practice of self-generating and creating *purpose*. You need to select specific goals to operationalize life, and little goals just aren't going to cut it. You need goals worth having in order to make the magic happen. It is intimidating to think large, but that's what you need to do.

If my goal is to publish this book then this may be intimidating, but only before I set to work on deconstructing the path.

There is a saying that asks, *"How do you eat an elephant?"*

The answer is, *"One bite at a time."*

First you need to identify or select "the elephant". If I remain with my example, the elephant-sized goal is to write this book. To sit down and begin writing an entire book is an intimidating task, but to simply create an outline is not intimidating at all. It is good fun to sort thoughts into different theoretical buckets which can later form chapter structure. It is also easy to then think of that chapter structure as a series of essays all of which are simply thoughts on particular topics. Another step is to ask myself *exactly when* I could write the chapters and how long it might take. At this point it helps to pull out a calendar and start allocating very *specific* timeslots to the activities.

This is not theoretical. If I actually allocate *specific* parcels of time, I can already tell you when this book will be finished? I am looking at a calendar now, which allocates Wednesday, December 11th, 2013 to the activity of building the outline and defining my tasks. December 12th is the next timeslot at which time my goal is to block out the specific additional writing sessions required to get to the finish line.

I have identified that I can write for an hour and a half each morning from 7:00am to 8:30am. If my chapter outlines are clear then to write a series of essays on particular topics is not overwhelming. Each chapter is simply an essay and each essay represents an unintimidating "bite" of the larger elephant (the book).

If I plot the "bites" on the calendar I can see that the underlying draft essays will be completed by Friday, December 20th. I have elected to take a leave day as well in order to create an *intensive* period which I can use to increase the pace or catch up in the event one of my previous sessions was a struggle. My strategic-self defined the elephant-sized goal and divided it into smaller bites for my execution-self to chew through. As long as I chew as planned, the draft manuscript will be finished before Christmas. Editing will be finalized by New Year's Eve. The final book will be published in the first week of January, 2014.

If you tell someone you are going to write a book then the "elephant-sized goal" seems overwhelming, but if you carve out the "bites" you begin to notice that each and every bite is chewable. This is a specific example, but it need not be. The same process of dividing elephants into bites can apply to any goal. You simply need to *plot those bites on the calendar*, and then commit to the act of chewing. Once you do this it becomes so empowering you'll wonder why you hadn't done it before. It's the simplest exercise in the world, and you'll go through your day knowing that you are on the road to something important.

Perfectionism is the enemy of *completion*

In this process be sure to prioritize *completion* over perfection. With large goals you need to be able to take decisions and progress at the appropriate pace. The inability to move forward can kill your goals. In the example of this book, I need to allocate time *later* for refining and editing. Permit yourself to make mistakes, but whatever you do, *press on*. You can fix mistakes, but if you can't move forward *with momentum* then your goals and dreams will die.

Sprints vs marathons

It is far easier to eat elephants in a series of *sprints* rather than in one long continuous marathon. The other day my wife asked me, *"Why don't you simply enjoy yourself and write a book over a longer period of time?"* The answer is that I believe the world is filled with long-distance marathon projects that either:

1) Never started because the project (and timeline) seemed too daunting, or

2) Never finish because passion fades before completion.

We either don't get started, or we start and lack the stamina to complete what we started. Hunger diminishes as you chew. This is a simple fact and the cure for this is to run *sprints*, not marathons. Eat hard and fast before your stomach knows how full you are. Work hard and fast so that by the time the early passion fades you can smell the finish line.

Passion is so valuable that you need to harness it while it's hot. When you design goals that require time that exceeds the life expectancy of your passion then you really run the risk of failing to complete. You only wake up at 5:30am to write a chapter of your book when you are *excited*. Once passion fades hard tasks generally become drudgery. If you have taken care to select goals aligned to your signature strengths then the lifespan of passion will be longer, but it's not infinite. Even a passionate writer can become tired of a particular project, for example. You need to harvest passion while it is fiery enough to fuel your goals, and to do this you need to condense them into *sprints* and power through to completion.

What if your goal is such a large elephant that it can't be condensed into a sprint? Simply divide the larger elephant-sized goal into smaller elephants and sprint through them one at a time. Completion is motivating. As you complete each goal you'll refill your reserves of passion and increase the odds of completing the overall objective.

Eat one elephant every year

I challenge the professionals I work with to have at least one elephant-sized goal each year. Ask yourself whether there is one particular goal you would like to accomplish over the course of the year. You want to be able to look back on the year and feel that you achieved something *truly* important and which helped you to grow. So what would satisfy this test for you? It needs to be inspiring enough to think that 12 months from now you'll be proud of having achieved it. That's your elephant.

Now ask yourself where *exactly* on the calendar this activity will live over the coming year. To do this effectively you should actually print a large calendar that you can look at and write on. Dissect the elephant into bites and put those bites on the calendar. Think in terms of the "time real estate" required and plot the real estate on the calendar.

Allow yourself to manage yourself

This is critical. Do not allow personal insubordination! If your strategic-self established a goal and allocated specific timeslots to a plan, then simply force your execution-self to deliver. At this stage, ensure you have given yourself the authority to govern yourself and kick your own butt out of bed if you have to. If you are *committed* in this way then once you've divided up your elephant into bites, the elephant is as good as chewed. You have effectively *already* accomplished your dreams and simply need to allow the inevitable to unfold.

Questions

Think about the following...

1) How often do you come up with seemingly good ideas, but don't get started because the overall project seems overwhelming?
2) How often do you get started on a goal but then lack the stamina and passion to complete it? Do some goals seem intoxicating at first, only to later yield to other priorities?
3) Do you divide your elephant-sized goals into specific, chewable bites? Do you allocate those bites to actual time real estate on your calendar?

Actions

What are you going to do with this information...

1) Take one of your elephant-sized goals and divide it into *very specific* bites.
2) Now pull out a calendar and ensure that you have *specific* time slots blocked out for chewing these bites.
3) Now strike while your passion is hot by *sprinting* forward. Don't make a plan that requires tiny amounts of time every day for the rest of your life. Your execution-self won't continue to deliver on the plan. Once passion fades, everything feels like "work". Run *sprints* (not marathons) with a full belly of passion and you'll accomplish more.

R. Sean Cochran

CHAPTER 7

VILLAGES AND VILLAGERS

"More business decisions occur over lunch and dinner than at any other time, yet no MBA courses are given on the subject."

- *Peter Drucker*

As we develop professionally, we gain certain skills and go to great lengths to refine them in order to be well suited to various careers. We tend to focus mainly on the *technical* skills behind professions. If we hope to be accountants we focus on accounting rules, if we aspire to be attorneys we focus on knowledge of law, and so on. This makes perfect sense, but once we have achieved the baseline technical skills necessary to pursue a career, it is often other more *interpersonal* factors that determine success. When these same professionals enter the workforce their accounting and legal skills are nearly taken for granted and are not likely the determining factors in career progression. The real differentiators for outlier professional success have far more social and interpersonal roots.

When your firm is considering whether to promote you, regardless of your resume or specific circumstances, one thing is certain in this decision process. *People* will make the final decision. A group of *people* will almost certainly sit down together in a room and discuss names on piece of paper. And *people* will decide.

Do you know exactly *which people* make these decisions about your future? Do they know you? When they see your name on that piece of paper what will they think? Could you get to know them?

This applies to almost every decision that matters for the attainment of your goals. *People* underlie decisions, and people are fundamentally social animals. Earlier in this book I addressed the perception of randomness in the world, and this is an area where we mistakenly attribute outcomes to chance. We actually have a great deal of variable control if we look at the world through the lens of *relationships*. Nearly any goal you would like to attain will involve a series of decisions made by *people*, and those people will either know, respect and like you, or they won't. *Relationship variables* are far more under your control than it seems and goal attainment without a relationship strategy is a mistake.

Relationship strategies cannot be implemented overnight. Much like a workout routine, if you expect to be thin after your first day at the gym then you've got a mistaken impression of how this works. You need to incorporate small activities into your daily life and the *aggregation* of these activities over time becomes a powerful force in your life. It establishes your "village".

Your village consists of the people in the world who know you and would be inclined to support you on various levels. There is an expression, "it takes a village to raise a child". I have two children and I know this to be true. It is also true for your career in that behind every CEO, Partner, Managing Director, or successful professional is an entire village of support. You may not see it, but it's there.

Don't leave the health of your village up to chance. Develop the daily, weekly, and yearly routines that cumulatively add up to a thriving village over time.

Network before you have needs

The day you desperately need someone's support, it's too late to offer up an invitation to lunch, drinks, or coffee. Take the time in advance to ask yourself who matters in your world. This is not a theoretical exercise, but rather a paper and pencil exercise. Are you able to define your village? There are obvious members, such as your clients, line manager, and direct colleagues. If you have not cultivated relationships with these individuals then now is a good time to start doing so, but more importantly have you considered extended networks? What about colleagues in other functions that support you? What about colleagues in other locations who hold roles you aspire to?

Take the time to map out your landscape in terms of relationships. Once you've done so, ask yourself whether you know these people and whether they know you? What specifically can you do in order to address the gaps? Having a relationship strategy seems straightforward, but in coaching various professionals I have found there is low hanging fruit here.

Establish a relationship strategy

Step 1:

Identify what your village should look like.

Step 2:

Who else do you need to bring into your village?

Step 3:

Mark your calendar with *specific* actions you will undertake.

There are few things more important than the pursuit of your dreams and every dream, personal or professional, can be made more likely to come true if you have a relationship strategy. However, in my experience this is rarely handled systematically and related actions are seldom *specifically* identified and placed on the calendar.

Consider mentors and mentees

Everyone benefits from having a mentor, and many of you will also find the act of being a mentor rewarding as well. These relationships serve a particular function in your overall relationship strategy.

When considering who might be an appropriate mentor, resist the temptation to select someone who is too directly connected to you commercially. It might seem convenient to have a mentor who will directly influence decisions about your career, but if the connection is *too* close then there are complications. I have served as mentor to certain individuals who later ended up reporting to me and the conflicts of interest posed a problem. The mentee likely felt encouraged by the fact that his mentor was now his manager, but my endorsement acquired a footnote, namely that I am the mentor and therefore conflicted. The endorsement of a known mentor risks being dismissed as biased.

Select a mentor who has certain skills you may want to acquire, or who has held roles that you aspire to. When you approach them you also want to place the burden of mentorship *on yourself* as mentee and not on the mentor. In other words, define what you are asking for and make it easy for the prospective mentor to accept. If mentorship means that you have a conversation once a month and pick the mentor's brain, then be sure to come prepared with topics to discuss. You are not asking the mentor to create a curriculum, but rather to simply show up as themselves.

Many senior professionals are not born educators and they may not have engaged in a mentoring relationship before. *Make it easy* and consider avoiding the use of the title "mentor" as well. If your request is to have a catch up on a regular basis so that you can have a sounding board to review some of your challenges, then it's easy for a mentor to commit. It's flattering and the preparation burden is, and should be, on you as the mentee.

Your broader village

How do you remember and potentially keep in touch with your more extended village? We all make new contacts every day and each person we meet could become a valuable member of our village. If you are like me, then you will never remember half of the names and details of the people you meet in life. Over the course of a career, the list is simply too long, and people change roles, firms, and sometimes countries. You need tools to support you, and if you are not already using social media, particularly LinkedIn, then you should strongly consider doing so.

LinkedIn is a social networking site that captures your professional information and allows you to "connect" with others and in turn see their professional information. It is dynamic in that so long as others update their information then you always have a current database for your extended village. This is valuable and efficient. You gain permanent recall of those already known to you and you are able to see interconnections for others not yet familiar.

If you already use LinkedIn, be sure to take it seriously. Headhunters, employers, and clients are likely to look you up and if someone "googles" your name then your LinkedIn profile will be amongst the search results. That's a good thing so long as your LinkedIn page represents you appropriately. Keep it professional and bear this visibility in mind.

You should also consider having a professional photo taken. I see a lot of LinkedIn profile photos that appear to be casually taken by a mobile phone. Sometimes these look fine, though typically they don't. Your profile is important so there's no reason not to invest in a headshot.

Also consider purchasing a book on building your LinkedIn profile. If you are new to the site then you won't be skilled at this and insight can only help. Just as it makes sense to ensure you have a highly professional resume, be sure to invest adequate time in your online presence. We now operate in a world in which others are more likely to review your LinkedIn profile than your printed resume. Keep this in mind.

Questions

Think about the following...

1) Do you employ deliberate relationship strategies?
2) Have you defined the people and relationships in your life of particular relevance to your goals?
3) How do you manage personal details for your contacts? Where do you keep this information and how do you update it?
4) Are you using LinkedIn or other social media? And how professional is your online presence?

Actions

What are you going to do with this information...

1) Categorize the current relationships in your life and devise a strategy for *systematic* contact.
2) Create a list of people you don't yet have a relationship with, but whom you'll need to know in order to achieve your goals.
3) Write down how you intend to get to know them, and *put a time on the calendar* for the activity you've described.
4) Professionalize your LinkedIn presence. If you are already active on LinkedIn then be sure to take your online presence seriously and consider seeking help with your profile to professionalize it.

R. Sean Cochran

CHAPTER 8

FEAR AND COURAGE

"I have learned that if one advances confidently in the direction of his dreams, and endeavors to live the life he has imagined, he will meet with a success unexpected in common hours."

- Henry David Thoreau

How you deal with fear is a major factor in your success. Most professionals are afraid of failure and even more fearful of the *appearance* of failure. Fear need not be your enemy, and properly harnessed it is a powerful motivator. However, fears are often exaggerated and unfortunately this causes many goals to be left unpursued.

Managing fear constructively

Fear is inevitable and if you are to engage constructively with that fear then you will need to get a handle on it. Here are a few steps to help manage fear constructively.

1) Assess the bites, and not the elephant

2) Determine what failure *really* looks like

3) When you elect to proceed, *commit*

Assess the bites, and not the elephant

We are usually intimidated by elephant-sized goals because we have not yet conceptualized how to divide the elephant into bite-sized pieces and created a process for chewing on them. If your dreams scare you then you may have simply failed to divide the steps into small enough steps. When frightened by your dreams, try dividing the parts further and further until the steps are no longer frightening.

Determine what failure *really* looks like

We tend to envision catastrophic versions of what failure looks like. Often these visions seem so terrible we eliminate the risk of failure by simply not pursuing the goal. If our vision of failure is irrational then we are robbed of our dreams.

When you elect to proceed, *commit*

We desperately want to feel successful *in the areas that matter* to us. The problem with this is that our minds tend to revise our view of what matters rather than face the prospect of *failure in something that matters*. We fail to commit upfront, or we revise history and interpret our failure as a sign that we must not have committed to begin with.

"If I had taken it more seriously the outcome would have been different."

"I simply haven't made it a priority."

Once you have dissected an elephant-sized goal into bite-sized chunks and you have assessed what failure really looks like, you need to *make a decision*. Are you going to take the risk, and are you going to *commit*. Don't get half-way in. Doing so will only reduce your odds of success and tenuous steps will set you up for failure.

Once you commit, you need to truly behave as though there's no other outcome in the world that you can envision. Put the finish line in your mind and schedule it on your calendar as the last stop in the plan. Victory has already happened and you're waiting for the scheduled hour to arrive. People who *commit* are simply more likely to win if they exude the confidence of a winner.

Lessons from rock climbing

I recall vividly when my wife, Angela, and I decided to pursue the sport of rock climbing and the lessons we learned in managing fear constructively.

To climb a large vertical rock pitch is a very intimidating goal when you look at the task from a distance without knowledge of the underlying equipment, techniques, and principles. When you have several hundred feet of air under your feet catastrophic failure seems to imply that you die. I suspect that this scenario leads most people to avoid the activity.

When you actually deconstruct rock climbing you begin to understand that the risks born by climbers are not what they seem. The equipment is incredibly advanced, the ropes and systems offer more protection than an onlooker may realize, and the variables are far more within one's control than a spectator understands. The prospect of climbing a mountain is an elephant-sized goal, though less intimidating when you understand and divide the bites.

A 300 foot climb is actually divisible into a series of 3 smaller 100 foot sections (aka "pitches"), and climbers don't embark on climbs at all without prior knowledge of the route. They are aware in advance of the relative difficulty as well as how feasible it is to protect oneself along the way. Route guides give this information in detail and climbers can pre-select climbs that are within their skill level and that are relatively straightforward to protect. And so the elephant begins to divide into bites. There are psychologically intimidating elements surrounding this activity, but many are less daunting than they seem and in reality the bites become quite chewable.

Don't get me wrong, rock climbing is an inherently dangerous activity. But so is driving in your car. A fundamental difference is that in your car you are no longer impressed by or afraid of the fact that you are traveling at 60 miles per hour. You understand the systems around you and you are able to divide the various elements of driving into smaller, unintimidating "bites". Likewise, being high off the ground in and of itself is psychologically interesting but not necessarily as fear-inspiring as it seems to be.

What if you fall?

In rock climbing I had maintained a terrible fear of falling *until I actually fell*. I was climbing a route together with my wife and recall being about 30 feet up when my footing slipped and I began to fall. Fear washed over me and I instantly plummeted 15 feet straight down. However, to my relief, Angela arrested the fall by stopping the rope as we had rehearsed and as the equipment is intended to function. I don't want to make a habit of falling, but I learned that *failure wasn't death*. Realistically, this was never what failure looked like, and I've since fallen several times and I'm still alive to write this chapter. Failure is not always pleasant, but it's not often catastrophic and *the expectation that it will be is not rational*.

Many of us fear that if we fail at work we'll be fired. Or we fear that we'll deliver a speech and the audience will laugh us off the stage or throw fruit. We fear that we won't be able to support our families and that we won't find opportunities in the future if we fail in our current goals. This simply isn't what failure really looks like.

Failure may not be pleasant, but it's rarely ever catastrophic. When you pursue a goal try to define what failure *really* looks like. If you accept a new job and it doesn't work out, will you end up destitute on the street unable to feed your family? As you consider an internal project, if it falls flat will people really ridicule you? If you leave your corporate job and launch something more entrepreneurial, will you be banned from future corporate opportunities forever? These depictions are simply not rationale to hold as your mental images of what failure looks like.

Courage

If you don't deconstruct the elephant and understand what failure really looks like then your courage needs to be impossibly high in order to pursue your goals. The fear you'll need to overcome will be irrational and crushing. Using my previous example, if you view the mountain in its entirety without deconstructing the climbing process then you'd have to be foolishly courageous to even start. Likewise, if you really view the base case failure scenario in climbing to be *death*, then again you need to be irrationally courageous to begin.

Once you view the tasks and the risks with clarity there remains a certain degree of risk that you cannot eliminate. This irreducible element should underlie the fear you evaluate and this is the degree of courage you need to muster up.

You don't need infinite reserves of courage, but at this stage you can't be hesitant if you want to maximize your chances of success. If you fail, then do so knowing that you boldly took a "good risk" and it went the other way. This isn't a tragedy and your ego will survive it! This happens and you'll live to fight again. Your colleagues and peers will also likely respect you all the more for having proceeded with courage and confidence.

Questions

Think about the following...

1) Do you have dreams that frighten you because pursuing them seems too risky?
2) How well have you deconstructed these elephant-sized dreams into bite-sized chunks? Are these smaller pieces still frightening?
3) Is your worst-case scenario really accurate? Are you sure that you know what failure looks like?
4) How strong are you in truly committing to your course of action once determined?

Actions

What are you going to do with this information...

1) Take an elephant sized goal and rather than fearing it in totality, deconstruct it and take inventory of the smaller bite-sized steps. They are likely far less frightening than the full-blown objective as a whole.
2) Now take the time to define what failure *really* looks like. You won't likely be living in a cardboard box unable to feed yourself if you are unable to succeed. What is a *realistic* base-case scenario should you fail to achieve your goal.
3) Now either *commit* to take the risk and drive forward, or decline the risk and walk away.
4) If you commit then burn the goal into your mind and envision the finish line so fully that you feel you've already won. Muster up the courage to be bold and move with confidence.

CHAPTER 9

RECORDING IN HD

"We fear that this moment will end, that we won't get what we need, that we will lose what we love, or that we will not be safe. Often our biggest fear is the knowledge that one day our bodies will cease functioning. So even when we are surrounded by all the conditions for happiness, our joy is not complete."

- Thich Nhat Hanh

The other day my 5 year old daughter, Madison, had an idea. *"Daddy, can we pleeeeease jump in the water at Redleaf?"*

I currently live in Sydney, Australia and near our home is a swimming area on the harbor called Redleaf Pool. It is surrounded by a wooden walkway that extends out into the water and forms a semicircle which serves as a border around the swimming hole. There are also a couple of floating wooden platforms in the middle of the swimming area and there is a small café on the shore near the beach. On a summer day it's a magical place for families.

"OK Madison, grab your swim suit. Let's go."

"Yeah!!", she yelled out, and she beamed excitement all the way there in the car.

When we got to Redleaf Pool the sky was sapphire blue and sure enough there were people everywhere with the same idea. Some were relaxing on the shore reading a book, some were out on the wooden walkway working up the courage to jump into the cold water, and some were swimming out to the floating platforms.

My five year old has not yet acquired the skill of patience nor has she developed the ability to "savor the moment". Madison immediately sprinted out on the walkway to prepare to jump in the water with Daddy. I walked along the platform behind her, catching up slowly but surely with her Olympic pace.

While walking I had the realization that this was one of the moments that *mattered*. It mattered a lot. In fact, I am quite sure that in the future, when I recall our time living in Sydney, I will remember a 5 year old girl sprinting in front of me begging Daddy to watch her jump.

What if I had failed to realize how much this moment mattered? What if I failed to pay attention? And what if my attention had been clouded with other thoughts and preoccupations?

Fortunately, I was truly paying attention that day. In fact I was trying to make a mental note to experience and record this event in *"high definition"* in my mind. There can't be any distractions. I need *to be there*, fully present, for a moment like that. Stressful work thoughts attempted to intrude for a moment and I realized how terrible it would have been to allow them to pollute the experience. I can get to work *later*.

You can only experience and record your life in "HD" when you are well and truly *there*. I was truly *there* that day.

Why we fail to be there

We all recall memories from our past and we also consider future events yet to happen, but we can only do so *now*. The "you" in the past lived these events in the present *at that time*. And the "you" in the future will also live events in the present when they eventually occur. Perhaps it goes without saying, but every experience happens *in the present*. Your ability to experience life *in the present* is the most important skill you have. You need to fully experience your best moments *as they are happening* and you need to prevent mental pollution from the past or future from impairing your ability to record and experience life in HD, *now*.

Paying attention to life as it unfolds *in the present* is difficult in practice because past stressful events have a way of turning themselves over and over in our minds. Likewise, we dwell on future *anticipated* stressful events, causing us to miss out on our present moment experience. Sometimes we manage to be in the present to some extent, but more or less as an outsider looking through a foggy glass window of past anxiety and future concerns. Our ability to direct our attention will fundamentally determine the quality of our experience, and therefore the quality of our lives.

Quarantine

To keep the past in perspective and the future constructive, we need to *quarantine* them both and keep them in their place. Earlier in the book I described carving elephant-sized goals into bite-sized chunks and then placing those bites into specific times on the calendar. This is a means of "*quarantine*".

The expected future creates anxiety *in the present* because we get overwhelmed by tasks not yet completed, conversations not yet held, and work not yet finished. This carving out of specific "time real estate" on your calendar is critically important, not only to your ability to accomplish goals but also to your ability to experience life more fully. You are not only quarantining specific *time* real estate, but also specific *mental* real estate. Do not welcome stress from the future before its scheduled appointment!

Many professionals I've coached do have certain tasks in quarantine, but they remain overwhelmed because there are quite a few "elephant bites" that have not yet been specifically allocated to the calendar. The uncertainty around completion of a task causes excessive dwelling on the future because at present your mind is not entirely confident in the steps. Your mind is not confident in the steps because you've not specifically defined and *scheduled* them. Your mind is no dummy and you need to do the work for the quarantine to be effective. Allocate *specific* calendar time. Once you've done so, you don't need to worry *now*. You have scheduled a specific time for that worrying.

When you fully embrace that you have a *specific* time quarantined for this, then you can more effectively focus on *now*. This also means that once the allocated time for chewing elephant bites arrives, you aren't still mentally swimming at Redleaf Pool. You'll need to commit to focused *execution* at the allotted time.

This process of enforcing mental quarantines will protect the boundaries of your experiences.

Savoring

What about future events that you *want* to dwell on and past events you *love* to recall? We only live in the present, but the act of reminiscing about wonderful past memories or exciting future prospects can enhance *the present*. If we experience and record life in HD, then being able to recall those memories is exactly the point.

The trouble with only living in the present (which is all we can ever do) is that it is infinitesimally fleeting and there's just no pause button! Being able to anticipate positive experiences, live through them in a fully present manner, and then reminisce about how wonderful they were boils down to *savoring*. If we cultivate our ability to deliberately savor the future, present, and past then our quality of life is immediately enriched.

Do others notice if do this?

I have a friend and colleague named Steve and there is something peculiar about the way he listens and the way he engages with others. I actually haven't seen Steve for years, but I came across another colleague who described him in a very particular way.

"He listens to you like you are the only person in the room."

I immediately felt that this was exactly correct and I was shocked that it was the first thing said about Steve by another person. Somehow he does this so effectively that I believe if you made this observation to anyone who knows Steve they would immediately nod their heads and agree. Somehow he is remarkable in this way.

Have you ever known someone like this? During most conversations others are listening to you, but there are a variety of distractions in any conversation. People look at you, they look at their surroundings, they notice their phone, they may notice the time, and they ruminate about something in their past and dwell on events to come in their future. But *sometimes it's different*.

Once in a while you speak to someone who is entirely there with you. They are clearly listening to your words, connecting with your meaning, looking at you, and unable to be shaken from the moment. They are *fully present*. People notice. You notice too. And it feels great to have someone *fully present* with you.

If I notice this in Steve, and everyone else notices this in Steve, what cumulative effect do you think this trait has over time? The impact *accumulates* over years of conversations and human interaction. Steve is an extremely successful individual and I suspect that this trait plays a part in that success.

Questions

Think about the following...

1) How often do you find that you are distracted during moments that *really* matter?
2) Do stressful thoughts about the past or future often diminish your important experiences in the present?
3) Do others have your *full* attention when you speak with them? Are you *fully* present as a listener? The people around you can tell the difference.

Actions

What are you going to do with this information...

1) Define stressful topics in the future and allocate *specific* time on the calendar when you will attend to them. Allocate time for deliberation, planning, and for execution. Once you've done so, treat the events as *quarantined* to these timeslots. During other times, they don't exist.
2) Realize the important parts of life *as they occur* and deliberately pay attention to experiencing them in the present. Ruminating about the past and dwelling on the future will only cloud your ability to experience moments *now*.
3) Learn to savor your experiences. Anticipate exciting events in the future, hold them fully in awareness as they occur, and linger on their memory as they recede into the past. Live life in "high definition".
4) Try listening to someone you care about like they are the *only* person in the room. Deliberately prepare yourself to do so beforehand and personally assess how well you do.

R. Sean Cochran

CHAPTER 10

SIMPLE STUFF

"Everything should be made as simple as possible, but no simpler."

- Albert Einstein

I want to let you in on something. Are you ready for it? There are no complex, secret formulas for success. If most of this book seemed simple, that's because it is. I even suspect you've learned many of these principles before, either in training programs or through another book on the topic of personal coaching or goal setting. Or perhaps, life has been your teacher.

The problem is not that we cannot find the secret formula to success. The challenge is that we *do* have the formula and we don't apply it in actual practice. All of life's most important lessons are actually very *simple*, and because they are simple we tend to look at them and say to ourselves, "I know this stuff". But we don't tend to *do* this stuff.

I hope that some of the principles in this book are useful and that they spark further insight for you, but really ask yourself whether you are *doing something with the information*. If I were your personal coach, I would now be asking you to describe what you intend to *do*. Your accomplishments and ultimately your well-being are derived from your *actions*. This is a book on *self*-coaching, so don't let yourself off too easy on this score.

Consider re-visiting the action items at the end of each chapter and assess whether you've *acted*. The simplest points are likely the most important points, yet when lessons seem straightforward we somehow become less likely to act. Keep your strategic-self hard at work in devising your action plans and ensure that your execution-self is pressed to deliver. Fundamentally, remember that *all* coaching is *self*-coaching and your dreams are depending on *you*. I wish you every success in the journey.

ABOUT THE AUTHOR

R. Sean Cochran is a Managing Director and sales division leader in a global financial institution. Sean has served as a sales, advisory, and business coach to hundreds of the world's top investment professionals in North America, Asia, and Australia. He currently resides in Sydney, Australia with his wife Angela and daughters, Madison and Olivia. Sean holds an MBA in Finance and Economics from Columbia Business School, a BA in Philosophy from Arizona State University, and is a Certified Financial Planner.

http://www.linkedin.com/in/rseancochran

www.ingramcontent.com/pod-product-compliance
Lightning Source LLC
Chambersburg PA
CBHW071753170526
45167CB00003B/1016